SCHOLASTIC

READING
SATs CHALLENGE
Year 2

Teacher's Guide

Scholastic Education, an imprint of Scholastic Ltd

Book End, Range Road, Witney, Oxfordshire, OX29 0YD

Registered office: Westfield Road, Southam, Warwickshire CV47 0RA

www.scholastic.co.uk

British Library Cataloguing-in-Publication Data

A catalogue record for this book is available from the British Library.

ISBN 978-1407-17549-2

Printed and bound by Ashford Colour Press

Author Charlotte Raby

Editorial Rachel Morgan, Audrey Stokes, Sarah Snashall, Shannon Keenlyside, Jennie Clifford

Cover and Series Design Neil Salt and Nicolle Thomas

Layout Neil Salt

Illustrations Adam Linley/Beehive Illustration, Young hippo (page 52) Trevorplatt/istock, Hippo charging (page 52) chuvipro/istock

Contents

About the book

This book is part of the *Scholastic SATs Challenge Programme*. It is designed to be used in conjunction with the *Skills Tests Papers* and *Workbook*.

The introduction provides overview information about how to support and challenge children in your school. This book has been written with different units which are numbered for ease-of-reference, but it is designed to work flexibly for your needs and does not need to be covered sequentially (see page 5 for more information). There are also a number of photocopiable resource sheets provided including an attendance chart, reward certificate and a letter for parents. A curriculum coverage overview, which allows you to locate specific needs easily is also provided.

Each unit follows the same structure. It is intended each session will take around 20 minutes and each unit could form multiple sessions, if required.

- **Objectives:** the objectives that the unit covers are provided.

- **What the children need to know:** a brief summary of the key points that the children need to know about the focus of the unit.

- **Test links:** test and question references to help you find related questions in the *Skills Test Papers* quickly.

- **Workbook links:** page references to the *Workbook* which relate to all or part of the unit.

- **Mastery and challenge ideas:** a range of challenging different ideas have been provided for each unit. It is not intended that all of these would be completed in a single session (or that all would need to be completed), rather that you would choose the most appropriate tasks for the children's needs.

- **Review:** suggestions on how to review and assess learning, including lines of questioning, example questions and short activities.

- **Watch and listen:** examples of learning to look and listen out for that may indicate mastery and depth of understanding of the topic.

At the end of the book are a range of photocopiable pages. These pages are generally linked to specific units and activities.

How to use *Challenge* in the classroom

Challenge has been designed to be used with children who are working at the expected standard and above. It is a mastery series which will work alongside your general class teaching.

All materials have been designed so they are initially accessible to most children but provide opportunity for stretch to those looking for and able to take on more of a challenge. It provides the flexibility to be used in a variety ways so you can choose which works best for you and your children.

As a **dip in/dip out whole-class resource** it can be used at any point during the year and leading up to the National Tests. The units in the *Teacher's Guide* have a topic focus that reflects National Curriculum objectives which makes them perfect to use through the year. Target the topics which need the most focused practice or choose a topic unit to provide additional challenge or deepen understanding. Children use the *Workbook* for individual practice and consolidation of ideas from the *Teacher's Guide*. The *Skills Test Papers* provides assessment opportunities and further practice children in test-style format. It includes eight reading texts which can be use across the year for challenging reading practice and assessment. Each reading text has accompanying questions which relate to areas of focus in the *Teacher's Guide*. They also closely match the style of question used in the National Curriculum Tests, so children will become familiar with the format of the tests and know what to expect.

You may also want to use the series to provide **small-group practice** for children working above expected standard or children who are working at expected standard but would benefit from additional challenge. Use it to provide challenging tasks and practice as part of your SATs preparation or, again, at any time throughout the year. The topic focus also allows you to group children by their areas of weakness or strength and target these specifically. This could mean that different groups of children are working on different topics at the same time. If you are using additional classes outside of school hours then you will need to ask parental permission; a letter template has been provided for this on page 15.

In a run-up to SATs, *Challenge* could also be used as a **twice weekly programme** used 8–12 weeks in advance of the National Tests. It is recommended that children take three of the practice tests from different genres at the beginning of the challenge programme and a fluency test to assess their knowledge and understanding. Work through the units in the *Teacher's Guide* consecutively or focus on areas in need of additional practice. Use the *Workbook* to support revision and practice. Use the reading texts and questions in the *Skills Test Papers* throughout for practice and assessment, perhaps using three of the tests at the mid-way point and three at the end, along with the second fluency test.

Whichever way you use the programme, you can use the *Teacher's Guide* for classroom ideas and support this with the activities in the *Workbook*. The *Skills Test Papers* can be used to identify areas to focus upon and to practise and consolidate learning.

Supporting and challenging more confident learners

All children need to be challenged and supported in their learning. For more confident learners, how is this best done? Will it look significantly different from other groups of learners?

With a mastery approach to learning, it should not be significantly different from one group of learners to another. With this in mind, do not limit these strategies to confident learners but make them available to all children, where appropriate.

Encourage a positive mindset

Foster a positive mindset among all children. It is not only children who are struggling who need to move away from a fixed mindset, in thinking they are not 'clever'. Children who see themselves as 'clever' may often resist engaging in tasks that are more challenging or where they think they may fail for fear of making mistakes, which would make them look and feel 'less clever'. This type of fixed mindset will limit children's progress, even if they are performing above expected levels. Tackle this by:

- Explaining to the children that it is through mistakes that we learn and encouraging them to take risks in their learning, such as aiming to read texts that are more challenging or of a genre they are less familiar with; asking demanding open-ended questions which do not have strictly 'correct' answers and expecting children to share their answers and explain their reasoning either orally or in writing. Read challenging texts aloud with unfamiliar vocabulary which children will struggle to understand or pronounce, so as to develop the habit of not always having it right in a context where they is no expectation to.

- Fostering an environment where mistakes are not only accepted but celebrated. Obviously, in a test setting this is not realistic but leading up to the National Tests and practising for them need not emphasise success based on a score. Praise sharing of errors and focus on the effort made and risk taken rather than having the correct answer. Ask, *Who got a different answer?* rather than asking *Who got that right?* Share work with 'interesting' errors with the class and encourage children to do the same. Work through questions together.

Learn deeply rather than moving on to 'harder' material

Allow time to look at topics and texts in depth, keeping children's interest by providing them with a wide range of tasks rather than giving them 'more of the same, but harder'. For example, in a lesson where you have been working on predicting what might happen next in a story on the basis has been read so far, ask them to identify a key point in the story or a character which, if they altered it slightly, would cause them to change their prediction and explain why.

The *Teacher's Guide* provides you with a variety of ideas and activities to choose from to keep children challenged and interested. Look for ways to extend and enhance both these and your own favourite activities. Many of the activity ideas and 'Watch and listen' points will offer suggestions on how to take a topic or activity further. Consider whether children could explore a topic more on their own. For example, comparing fairy-tale female characters to those in traditional tales in stories from around the world. You may also wish to use the *Workbook* to provide additional practice which children could move on to independently once they have completed an activity.

Apply learning to real-life experiences

Being able to apply what they have learned in both familiar and new situations will stretch and motivate children. Real-life contexts will provide greater meaning to many topics and demand children use a variety of skills across topics and subjects which otherwise may seem disconnected from everyday life. For example, a meaningful non-fiction reading task will demonstrate how grammar, punctuation and vocabulary used effectively (or perhaps ineffectively) will convey meaning successfully. This will embed the learning and lead to deeper understanding. Look for opportunities around the home and school, such as publicity for upcoming local events or performances aimed at children, asking children to summarise main ideas, identify key details, considering how artwork is used and how text is organised for effect. They could then create their own publicity for an upcoming school event.

Encourage reflection and exploration through discussion

Most National Test questions will not ask children to explain their thinking but being able to do this will deepen their understanding and bring to light any areas of misconception which can quickly be addressed; both of which will have an overall positive impact on their learning as well as test results. More confident learners may be able to answer a question quickly but this will not necessarily be an indicator of depth of knowledge. Expect children to dig deeper by encouraging them to explain not only what they know but how they know it. Use open-ended questions to get children talking.

Provide opportunities for children to reflect, explore and discuss what they know across subjects and throughout the day. Below are a few strategies and examples for getting children reasoning and talking about reading.

- Give children two less-familiar traditional tales to read and ask them to tell you what is the same or different about them.
  - ○ Children will notice, depending on the stories chosen, similarities and differences in plot, the use of clearly 'good' and 'evil' characters and recognise simple examples of recurring language, for example *Once upon a time*. They will able to explain their answers confidently.
- Make a statement and then ask the children to consider, based on this statement and their knowledge of the wider topic, *What else do we know?*

  A compound word is a word made of two separate words, for example lighthouse.

  - ○ Children might begin by talking about what a compound word is, what the two individual words mean compared to the compound word. They may identify other compound words and offer examples.
- Make a statement and ask children to consider if it is sometimes, always or never true. Ask them to provide examples to support their thinking.

  All plays need a narrator.

  - ○ Children will confidently discuss key elements of a play and use plays they have seen or read as examples to support their thinking.

Achieving and identifying mastery

In simple terms, **mastery** can be defined as: *comprehensive knowledge or skill in a particular subject or activity.*

It follows that a child with a higher level of mastery will not only have a deep understanding of a subject but score higher in the National Tests than a child with a lower level, even if they know the same content.

With this is in mind, how can you achieve and identify mastery with greater depth with the *SATs Challenge* programme?

Achieving mastery

The mastery and challenge activities in this *Teacher's Guide* offer a variety of engaging activities to choose from. Aim to include a range of activities to develop children's reading fluency and reasoning skills. Photocopiable materials provide further practice. The *Workbook* gives children further practice in each topic and allows them to consolidate their learning and deepen their understanding.

For each subject, how to ensure mastery will require slightly different strategies which are outlined in each activity in the *Teacher's Guide* however, across all subjects: provide opportunities for children to explain their thinking and to use what they have learned previously and to apply in new situations; encourage a steady but deep pace, rather than rushing on to a new topic; apply learning to real-life experiences where possible, and show its purpose; and aim for more 'children's voice' than 'teacher's voice', encouraging them to explain their thinking and explore topics thoroughly.

Identifying mastery

What will mastery at greater depth look like?

For example, if the learning objective is to predict what might happen in a story on the basis of what they have read so far, children demonstrating mastery would be able to recognise implied meaning in the story with ease. They would be able to explain their reasoning and elaborate confidently on what may happen next and how the story may develop. They would be able to predict how the story would change if it were told from another character's point of view.

How do I identify it?

The tests in the *Skills Test Papers* can be used not only to quickly assess children's understanding of a topic before or after reviewing but, by looking at a specific question in depth, provide an excellent starting point for an assessment of depth of mastery of a topic or objective. For example, for the test question below the correct answer is 'her father'. Follow-up questions you could use to assess depth of mastery might include: *How do we know that she is eager for her father to come home? In the first paragraph, how do you think Ashputtel is feeling? How do you know? Think about what words you could use to replace 'screeching' in the first sentence and 'sighed' in the second to make the reader think that Ashputtel is happy. Does this story remind you of any stories you have read before? How are they similar? How are they different?*

1. Ashputtel could hear her stepsisters screeching upstairs. She leaned on her broom and sighed. When would her father come home?

Who was Ashputtel waiting for?

Each unit in this *Teacher's Guide* has a series of 'Watch and listen' points which describe what mastery at greater depth might look like in relation to the topic covered. Keep these points in mind when working through activities as well as when children are working independently in the *Workbook*. Ask them to explain their thinking as they work and extend practice questions with further questioning.

Working at greater depth

Below are two tables that list the National Curriculum objectives for word reading and comprehension. The objectives have been broken down to indicate what children should be demonstrating if they are working at greater depth in these areas. Use this list as another tool to help you track and assess children's mastery of a topic and depth of understanding.

Word reading

National curriculum objective	Working at greater depth
Continue to apply phonic knowledge and skills as the route to decode words until automatic decoding has become embedded and reading is fluent.	Fluently reading age-appropriate texts, reading aloud with competence.
Read accurately by blending the sounds in words that contain the graphemes taught so far, especially recognising alternative sounds for graphemes.	Read age-appropriate texts accurately and fluently, knowing when to use alternative sounds for graphemes.
Read accurately words of two or more syllables that contain the same graphemes as above.	Can accurately read a wide range of words of three or more syllables.
Read words containing common suffixes.	Can read many words containing common suffixes, and understand how they are formed.
Read further common exception words, noting unusual correspondences between spelling and sound and where these occur in the word.	Can read quickly and accurately a wide range of common exception words beyond those taught in Year 2.
Read most words quickly and accurately, without overt sounding and blending, when they have been frequently encountered.	Can read words in books at a reading age higher than their chronological age accurately and fluently without overt sounding and blending at over 90 words per minute.
Read aloud books closely matched to their improving phonic knowledge, sounding out unfamiliar words accurately, automatically and without undue hesitation.	Can sound out most unfamiliar words in books at a reading age higher than their chronological age accurately, without undue hesitation.
Re-read these books to build up their fluency and confidence in word reading.	Can confidently read aloud familiar books at a reading age beyond their chronological age.

Comprehension

National curriculum objective	Working at greater depth
Listen to, discuss and express views about a wide range of contemporary and classic poetry, stories and non-fiction at a level beyond that at which they can read independently.	Can offer thoughtful and explained comments about a range of texts and can listen and respond to the views of others.
Discuss the sequence of events in books and how items of information are related.	Can explain the plot of a story or structure of a non-fiction book they have read independently and can display an understanding of cause and effect.
Become increasingly familiar with and retelling a wider range of stories, fairy stories and traditional tales.	Can retell with drama and adapt own versions of familiar stories.
Be introduced to non-fiction books that are structured in different ways.	Can explain the structure and purpose of a range of non-fiction texts structured in different ways.
Recognise simple recurring literary language in stories and poetry.	Can provide examples of recurring literary language that they have encountered.
Discuss and clarify the meanings of words, linking new meanings to known vocabulary.	Can understand, remember and use new words encountered in reading.
Discuss their favourite words and phrases.	Can discuss their favourite words and phrases in books they read independently.
Continuing to build up a repertoire of poems learned by heart, appreciating these and reciting some, with appropriate intonation to make the meaning clear.	Can create a clear and dramatic solo performance of a few short poems known by heart.
Draw on what they already know or on background information and vocabulary provided by the teacher.	When reading independently, can draw on what they already know or on background information and vocabulary provided by the teacher.
Check that the text makes sense to them as they read and correct inaccurate reading.	In a book they are reading independently, can check that the book makes sense and correct inaccurate reading.
Make inferences on the basis of what is being said and done.	In a book they are reading independently, can make inferences on the basis of what is being said and done.
Answer and ask questions.	In a book they are reading independently, can answer questions about the text and ask their own questions about the text that they do not know the answer to.
Predict what might happen on the basis of what has been read so far.	In a book they are reading independently, can predict what might happen on the basis of what is being said and done.
Participate in discussion about books, poems and other works that are read to them and those that they can read for themselves, taking turns and listening to what others say.	Can provide thoughtful opinions about texts they have read. Can take turns in a discussion and build on the ideas of others.
Explain and discuss their understanding of books, poems and other material, both those that they listen to and those that they read for themselves.	Eloquently explain and discuss their understanding of books, poems and other material, both those that they listen to and those that they read for themselves.

Objective coverage overview

Unit	Objectives
1 Checking for sense	To check that the text makes sense to them as they read and correct inaccurate reading. To read most words quickly and accurately, without overt sounding and blending, when they have been frequently encountered.
2 What words mean: prefixes	To discuss and clarify the meanings of words, linking new meanings to known vocabulary. To draw on what they already know or on background information and vocabulary provided by the teacher.
3 Compound words	To discuss and clarify the meanings of words, linking new meanings to known vocabulary. To draw on what they know or on background information.
4 Reading homophones	To discuss and clarify the meanings of words, linking new meanings to known vocabulary. To draw on what they know or on background information. To distinguish between homophones and near-homophones.
5 What words mean: synonyms	To discuss and clarify the meanings of words, linking new meanings to known vocabulary. To draw on what they already know or on background information and vocabulary provided by the teacher. To draw on knowledge of vocabulary to understand texts.
6 Shades of meaning	To read accurately most words of two or more syllables. To discuss and clarify the meanings of words, linking new meanings to known vocabulary. To draw on knowledge of vocabulary to understand texts.
7 Reading accurately	To read aloud books closely matched to their improving phonic knowledge, sounding out unfamiliar words accurately, automatically and without undue hesitation. To re-read these books to build up their fluency and confidence in word reading. To check that the text makes sense to them as they read and to correct inaccurate reading. To read accurately words of two or more syllables.
8 Reading punctuation and dialogue	To check that the text makes sense to them as they read and to correct inaccurate reading. To make inferences on the basis of what is being said and done. To read most words quickly and accurately, without overt sounding and blending, when they have been frequently encountered.

Objective coverage overview

Unit	Objectives
9 The features of fiction	To answer and ask questions. To discuss their understanding of books, poems and other material.
10 Retelling stories	To retell a wider range of stories, fairy stories and traditional tales. To understand the books they read by drawing on what they already know or on background vocabulary.
11 Sequencing stories	To discuss the sequence of events in books and how items of information are related. To explain and discuss their understanding of books. To predict what might happen on the basis of what has been read so far.
12 Making links to other books	To make links between the book they are reading and other books they have read. To understand the books they read by drawing on what they already know or on background information.
13 Making predictions	To predict what might happen on the basis of what they have read so far. To become familiar with fairy stories and traditional tales. To make inferences on the basis of what is being said and done.
14 Understanding description	To recognise simple, recurring literary language in stories and poetry.
15 Inference: what characters say, do and think	To make inferences on the basis of what is said and done.
16 Fiction: your opinion	To express views about a wide range of contemporary and classic poetry, stories and non-fiction.
17 Reading non-fiction	To be introduced to non-fiction books that are structured in different ways. To answer and ask questions. To discuss their understanding of books, poems and other material.
18 Links in non-fiction	To understand how items of information are related.
19 Making an explanation: fiction and non-fiction	To explain and discuss their understanding of books, poems and other material.

Progression chart

Name: _____

Unit		Skills checked	Practised	Aimed higher!
1	Checking for sense			
2	What words mean: prefixes			
3	Compound words			
4	Reading homophones			
5	What words mean: synonyms			
6	Shades of meaning			
7	Reading accurately			
8	Reading punctuation and dialogue			
9	The features of fiction			
10	Retelling stories			
11	Sequencing stories			
12	Making links to other books			
13	Making predictions			
14	Understanding description			
15	Inference: what characters say, do and think			
16	Fiction: your opinion			
17	Reading non-fiction			
18	Links in non-fiction			
19	Making an explanation: fiction and non-fiction			

Attendance chart

Subject: _____ Teacher: _____

Name	1	2	3	4	5	6	7	8	9	10	11	12	13	14	15	16	17	18	19

Dear Parents and Carers,

As you will be aware, towards the end of Year 2, the children will be sitting their National Curriculum (SATs) tests. This is obligatory for all children attending state schools and this year the tests will be taking place from _____ to _____. The tests the children will be sitting are:

English: Spelling – around 15 minutes

English: Grammar and Punctuation – around 20 minutes

English: Reading, two papers – around 30 minutes and 40 minutes each

Mathematics: Arithmetic – around 20 minutes

Mathematics: Reasoning – around 35 minutes

The purpose of the tests is to monitor and compare the performance of state schools, but also to check on the abilities and progress of each child. Scores may continue to be used in Key Stage 2 as a benchmark for future performance.

We are planning a series of Challenge sessions we would like your child to attend, if possible. These sessions will focus on deepening your child's understanding in a variety of areas and provide an opportunity for stretch and challenge. As such, the focus of these sessions will not generally be on explicit test practice. However, deep understanding and strong reasoning skills will be very beneficial when taking the tests.

Subject: _____

Dates: _____

Day(s): _____

Times: _____

If you are happy for your child to attend, please complete the form below and return it to us.

The best way to support your child through this period is to ensure that they get plenty of sleep and exercise, ensure they are not unduly worried about the tests, and that when they are doing homework they have a calm and quiet environment to work in. If you feel the need to do additional work with your child, please speak to us first so that we can work together and avoid duplication or confusion.

If there is anything else you would like us to clarify or provide further information on, please let us know.

With thanks for your support,

The Year 2 team

- -

Year 2 Challenge sessions

Child's name: _____

I give my permission for my child to attend the Challenge sessions.

Name: _____ Signed: _____

MSCHOLASTIC

Reward Certificate

Well done!

I've aimed higher with SATs Challenge

Name: _____ Date: _____

My strongest areas are:

_____

_____

I will challenge myself to fly higher in:

_____

1 Checking for sense

Objectives

- To check that the text makes sense to them as they read and correct inaccurate reading.
- To read most words quickly and accurately, without overt sounding and blending, when they have been frequently encountered.

What the children need to know

- How to read without undue hesitation so they can look ahead as they read.
- The meanings of most common words.
- To stop and think when a word they read seems out of place or is unknown.

TEST LINKS:

Test 1: Q1, 2, 4, 5, 6, 7, 8, 9, 10, 11
Test 2: Q1, 3, 4, 6, 7, 8, 10, 11
Test 3: Q1, 2, 3, 14, 15, 16
Test 4: Q1, 7
Test 5: Q1, 2, 5, 6
Test 6: Q1, 2
Test 7: Q1, 4
Test 8: Q1, 2, 4, 6

WORKBOOK LINKS:
Pages 6–10

✎ Challenge and mastery ideas

- Ensure that children are reading each word accurately when reading aloud.
- Check that the children have understood what they read by making a statement that they can agree or disagree with, for example: *I think the boy was scared when he got in the boat.* Use this as a basis for any further teaching of misconceptions about language or for general comprehension.
- Use sentences with red herring words, such as those on page 7 of the *Workbook*, to check that the children are monitoring their reading and can think about what they are reading as they read.
- Write sentences and non-sentences for the children to read. Help them understand why a non-sentence (such as, *I can see wild*) does not make sense. Work together to create a sentence that makes sense.
- Children need to be reading at least 90 words per minute. Use Fluency Test 1 in the *Skills Test Papers* to work out children's reading speed. (See page 23 for advice about fluency.)
- Children need to monitor what they read to become fluent readers. Often, as children gain reading speed they lose accuracy. Encourage children to look ahead as they read so they can start to think about what words are coming next. Watch for children's eyes flicking ahead as they read.

✎ Review

- Listen to the children as they read a passage with tricky language (for example an excerpt from 'Dark is fun' from *The Owl Who Was Afraid of the Dark* by Jill Tomlinson). Ensure that the children think carefully about what they're reading as they read (for example, ask: *Why does Plop fall out of the tree? What has happened to Scumbo? Why is the boy sitting by the fire? What is the roly-poly pudding?*)

✎ Watch and listen

- Listen for children who can read fluently and accurately.
- Listen for children who can accurately discuss the content of what they have read, picking up on easily missed details.
- Watch for children who can concentrate on what they are reading and can become absorbed in the text.
- Watch for children who can accurately spot errors in their own and classmates' writing, correcting any errors they find.

2

Objectives

- To discuss and clarify the meanings of words, linking new meanings to known vocabulary.
- To draw on what they already know or on background information and vocabulary provided by the teacher.

What the children need to know

- What a root word is.
- That when a prefix is added to a root word, the meaning of the word changes.

WORKBOOK LINKS:

Pages 11–13

What words mean: prefixes

◢ Challenge and mastery ideas

- Extend the children's understanding of prefixes that combine with the root word to make the opposite meaning. The children will have encountered the prefix 'un', but will meet many of the other prefixes that create negatives as they read. (Note, the curriculum only requires Year 2 children to know the prefix 'un', introducing other prefixes should be done from a understanding what they are reading perspective so as not to move into future year's work.)

- Write a list of words that have negative prefixes for example: *untruth, unbelievable, impossible, impolite, inactive, incautious, disagree, disallow, nonsense, non-stick.* Ask the children to look at these words and encourage them to notice that there are two or three letters (prefixes) added to another word (a root word).

- Ask questions that encourage children to make connections between the root word and its changed meaning, for example: *How are the words 'possible' and 'impossible' connected?* Use examples in sentences and explore how the meaning changes.

◢ Review

- Ensure the children use their knowledge of prefixes when answering vocabulary questions. Remind them to read the word correctly, understanding any change made to the root word.

- Provide the children with photocopiable page 38 'Root word challenge'. Ask the children to cut up each word into root word and prefix. Ask them to talk explicitly about the job that prefixes do, and how they alter the meaning of the root word. Challenge them to create new words with their root words and the prefixes (they won't be able to make many but they might find: *unbalance, unbelief, unlike* and *unarm*). Note, the words on the photocopiable page are deliberately challenging, you could provide a different set of words if you prefer.

◢ Watch and listen

- Watch out for children with a curiosity about new vocabulary. Foster a sense of excitement about discovering new words that they can add to their growing understanding of the English language.

- Children who understand that the meaning of a word changes when a prefix is added to a root word will be able to speedily make connections to the meaning of words as they read. This will help them become fluent readers with accurate comprehension.

3 Compound words

Objectives

- To discuss and clarify the meanings of words, linking new meanings to known vocabulary.
- To draw on what they know or on background information.

What the children need to know

- That some words are made up of two words added together to make a new word.
- How to identify the two or more words that make up the new word.
- How to use the meaning of the individual words to work out what the new word means.

WORKBOOK LINKS:

Pages 14–17

✈ Challenge and mastery ideas

- Clarify that joining two words together, often two nouns, creates a new word called a compound word. Explain that many common words have been made this way. The meaning of the new word usually brings together attributes of the two words: a *bedroom* is a room with a bed in it.
- Compound words are often created to describe a new thing and because new things are often improved upon and replaced with even newer things, they can get left behind. For example, these days 'greenhouse' is used more than 'glasshouse'. Provide the children with a list of old compound words and challenge them to help you work out their meaning from the two original words, for example: *laserdisc*, *Walkman*, *videocassette*, *cutpurse* (pickpocket), *fourscore* (you might want to tell them that 'score' means 20), *otherwhere* (elsewhere), *sweetmeat* (a sweet treat).
- Some pronouns are compound words as well: *yourself*, *myself*, *everybody*, and so on. Show children how these words are created and check they understand what the words mean. Remind children how word families work and help them create pronoun word families: for example, the 'self' family: *myself*, *yourself*, *ourselves*, *itself* and so on.
- New compound words are created all the time to name new things. Challenge the children to make up new compound words for inventions of their own (*roomtidier*, *homeworkmaker*, and so on).

✈ Review

- Ensure that the children are spotting new compound words as they encounter them and are using the correct process to work out the meaning.
- Provide the children with photocopiable page 39 'Compound words'. Observe the children as they locate and use the two words that create the compound word to understand and explain its meaning.

✈ Watch and listen

- Watch for children who can use knowledge of compound words to unpick unfamiliar vocabulary, for example, old-fashioned language that includes unusual compound words such as *hereinafter* and *albeit*. Can they work out what are the root words and how they work together to create a new word?
- Listen for children who can incorporate compound words they have encountered into their own vocabulary.

4

Reading homophones

Objectives

- To discuss and clarify the meanings of words, linking new meanings to known vocabulary.
- To draw on what they know or on background information.
- To distinguish between homophones and near-homophones.

What the children need to know

- Words can have more than one meaning depending on the context.
- Some words sound the same, but have different meanings and spellings.

WORKBOOK LINKS:

Pages 18–19

✈ Challenge and mastery ideas

- Make links to homophones the children have learned in spelling lessons: any study of homophones will, by its nature, combine reading and spelling. Explore further common homophones and ensure that the children know their meanings.

- Spend time on clarifying the most common and most troublesome homophones, such as the particularly tricky *it's* and the possessive pronoun *its* and *they're*, *their* and *there*. Draw the children's attention to the words surrounding these words to help them understand the job each word is doing in the sentence.

- Use images and word association to help children cement meaning and spelling, for example, *I hear with my ear*. Make links between the word, image and its spelling to help children remember its meaning. For example:

son

sun

- Hold up a range of homophones on flashcards (for example, the words on photocopiable page 40 'Homophones' enlarged for class use). With each word, challenge the children to quickly turn to a partner and either explain the meaning of the word or use the word in a sentence.

✈ Review

- Use photocopiable page 40 'Homophones' to check the children's understanding of key homophones.

✈ Watch and listen

- Watch out for children who quickly understand homophones from context as they read, as this ensures accurate comprehension.
- Listen to children who can quickly understand the meaning of a homophone out of context through spelling alone.

5

What words mean: synonyms

Objectives

- To discuss and clarify the meanings of words, linking new meanings to known vocabulary.
- To draw on what they already know or on background information and vocabulary provided by the teacher.
- To draw on knowledge of vocabulary to understand texts.

What the children need to know

- That different words can have similar meanings.
- How to read the clues in a text to work out a new word.
- How to link a new word to words they already know.

✈ Challenge and mastery ideas

- Explain that many words in the English language have similar meanings. Note that children do not need to know the term 'synonym' at this stage, but you may introduce the term if you feel it is appropriate.
- Ask the children to discuss all the different words they know that mean 'big'. Listen to the children's ideas, writing each one on a sticky note, for example: *large, huge, great, gigantic, massive* and so on.
- Ask the children to help you order the words along a 'line of intensity,' from smallest to biggest. Ask the children to give a reason for their choice of order. Ensure they understand there isn't a perfect order, but that each word has a slightly different meaning.
- Repeat this activity for other groups of synonyms, for example, words that mean: small (*tiny, minute, little, pocket-sized*), amazing (*fantastic, epic, brilliant, great, wonderful, very good, excellent*), beautiful (*pretty, sweet, lovely, handsome, nice*), brave (*courageous, heroic, bold, fearless*), delicious (*tasty, yummy, mouth-watering*) and so on.
- Help children make links between the synonymous words that you explore by using the words in context.
- Provide the children with copies of photocopiable page 41 'Synonym snap'. Organise for them to use the cards to play 'synonym snap' or 'synonym pairs'. Tell them that a 'snap' or a 'pair' is two words with similar meanings.
- Create word-web displays that show how words are connected by meaning.

✈ Review

- Ask the children to read a passage looking for specific synonymous words, for example, words linked to happiness, noise or speech, depending on those used in the passage. Discuss with the children why each word was used and how the different synonyms change the meaning in the sentence.

✈ Watch and listen

- Watch out for children who understand that although words can be synonyms, they don't always replace each other in every context. For example *cold, freezing, chilly* and *cool* have slightly different meanings. To explore this further, ask the children which of the words could describe the weather and which could be used to describe a character.
- Look out for children who can understand the shades of meaning created by synonyms as they will be able to accurately imagine what they read.

6

Shades of meaning

Objectives

- To read accurately most words of two or more syllables.
- To discuss and clarify the meanings of words, linking new meanings to known vocabulary.
- To draw on knowledge of vocabulary to understand texts.

What the children need to know

- That words can have similar meanings.
- How to link a new word to words they already know.
- That writers choose the best word to convey what they want to say.

TEST LINKS:

Test 1: Q4, 6, 7, 8
Test 2: Q1
Test 3: Q14
Test 4: Q7, 8
Test 5: Q2, 4, 7
Test 7: Q1, 4
Test 8: Q2, 4, 8

WORKBOOK LINKS:
Pages 23-25

Challenge and mastery ideas

- In order to build their vocabulary, children need practice in using synonyms and understanding how different words can be used in different situations.
- Help children to explore the meaning of words by playing a categorising game. Say: *Which of these things can be ferocious? If I say something that is ferocious, you shout: 'Angry Bear!'. If I say something that isn't ferocious, whisper: 'Mouse!'*. Say the following phrases, pausing for the children to shout their response: *a lion hunting, an otter playing, a shark attacking, a sprinter running, children laughing, a wolf pack howling* and so on.
- Repeat the game with other words such as *magnificent, delicate, eerie, disappointing, precious*.
- Collect words and phrases that could be used in different settings. Challenge the children to use exact language, including adjectives, that applies to the setting. For example, these descriptions could all describe a school environment: *bright, cheerful corridors; a bustling, noisy playground; a world full of books in the library*. Make word webs about the settings together and display them.
- Explain that some words are very adaptable and can be used to describe many things, for example, a person could be *splendid* as could a place or a thing. However, a place can be *eerie* but a person cannot. Use photocopiable page 42 'The right word' to help children distinguish between words that are used to describe people and things. If the children are struggling, suggest that they test out words in the following sentences:

  The girl was _____.

  It was a _____ castle.

Review

- Provide the children with a series of similar sentences and ask them to discuss the slight difference in the meaning of each one with a partner. For example:

  The fast car.

  The sports car.

  The racing car.

  The expensive car.

Watch and listen

- Watch out for children who understand that synonymous words are subtly different. Ask the children questions such as: *Which word shows greater fear: terrified or frightened?*
- Look out for children who have an understanding of how more unusual or unrelated words could be connected as this shows a deeper understanding of how language works.

7

Reading accurately

Objectives

- To read aloud books closely matched to their improving phonic knowledge, sounding out unfamiliar words accurately, automatically and without undue hesitation.
- To re-read these books to build up their fluency and confidence in word reading.
- To check that the text makes sense to them as they read and to correct inaccurate reading.
- To read accurately words of two or more syllables.

What the children need to know

- How to use their phonic knowledge to accurately read most words.
- Sound out unknown words and blend them speedily.
- How to break up words into syllables, read each sound in each syllable in order and then blend the whole word.

TEST LINKS:

Test 1: Q1, 6, 7, 8
Test 2: Q1, 3
Test 3: Q14, 15
Test 5: Q2, 4, 7

WORKBOOK LINKS:
Pages 26–29

✈ Challenge and mastery ideas

- Reading accurately is a skill; it takes practice to master and needs to be modelled. Explain to the children that when they are reading accurately it should sound like they are talking. Model reading a text in a 'robot voice' at about one word per second. Ask the children to 'coach' you by telling you how to improve your reading. Take their feedback and re-read the text until you are reading with a natural speaking voice. Do not overdo the expression!

- Ask the children to read a couple of pages of text to their partner. Tell the partner that they are the reading coach and need to give precise feedback to their partner to help them read accurately with a natural speaking voice. Get the children to swap roles and repeat reading the same bit of text a few times each until they feel that they are reading with accuracy.

- Choose extracts of texts or poems to read chorally. Read the text to the children first, discuss any words that are tricky and ensure the children understand the meaning of all the words. Invite the children to join in and read the text with you. Try to read at an even pace.

- Using a book from a class set, read a passage to the children as they follow in their own copies. Tell the children that you are going to miss out words or phrases and they should join in and read the missing words. Challenge the children to join in without hesitation.

- Try some or all of the following activities to increase fluency and accuracy:
  - Regular partner reading; re-reading a short text (100 words) until it is effortless.
  - Reading and re-reading poetry, thinking about how the poem sounds, so that the listener can enjoy the rhythm and rhyme.
  - Record children reading a picture book for younger children to enjoy. Explain that they need to read at a steady, even speed so the listener can follow along and enjoy the story.
  - Choose texts that the children can read at 90 per cent accuracy. These will need to be more complex books for children working at greater depth. This means that the children should be able to read most of the text without hesitation and only need to work out one in ten words.

- Focus on reading multisyllabic words. Provide the children with copies of photocopiable page 43 'Syllable snips'. Ask the children to read each word and mark the number of syllables in each word.

- Ask the children to draw a vertical line at the end of each syllable. Ask them to circle any graphemes that they are unsure of, for example, /sh/ represented by the graphemes 'ssi', 'ti', and /zh/ represented by 'si' and 'ci'.
- Teach the children how to speedily read multisyllabic words by:
    ○ recognising the root word
    ○ recognising the two words that make up a compound word
    ○ breaking the words up and blending each chunk in turn, then reading the word all the way through
    ○ reading two-syllable words and then working up to three- and four-syllable words
    ○ practising reading words that they have identified as tricky until they are fluent.

 Review

- Use individual reading sessions to identify any graphemes that the children are unsure of. Teach these explicitly. Children often hesitate over the various spellings of the long-vowel sounds.

Watch and listen

- Watch out for children who read smoothly, working out new words quickly without needing to overtly sound them out.
- Watch out for children who can read complex words fluently and accurately.

8

Reading punctuation and dialogue

Objectives

- To check that the text makes sense to them as they read and to correct inaccurate reading.
- To make inferences on the basis of what is being said and done.
- To read most words quickly and accurately, without overt sounding and blending, when they have been frequently encountered.

What the children need to know

- What punctuation means and how to use their voice to show the punctuation.
- How to use cues in the text to give the right expression when reading dialogue.
- How to make inferences about characters and show this in how they read dialogue or stress certain words in a text.

WORKBOOK LINKS: Pages 30–32

◢ Challenge and mastery ideas

- Ensure the children understand the function of each type of punctuation. Show the children how to read an ellipsis by slowing your voice as you reach the ellipsis and then pausing before starting the next sentence with a different tone.

- Use the sentences on photocopiable page 44 'With feeling' to explore sentences with exclamations. Tell the children that the exclamation mark tells you that these sentences have been written 'with feeling' but, in order to read them with the correct expression, they need to think carefully about the feeling that the writer is trying to convey. Ask the children to discuss the feeling of each sentence and write it on the line. Tell them to take turns reading the sentences to their partner. Can the partner work out which feeling they are trying to convey?

- For an added challenge, teach the children how to read an aside in the text (parenthesis). This is commonly marked by two commas, brackets or dashes.

- Choose some dialogue from a familiar story. Show the children how the words directly after the dialogue often tell you how it should be spoken. Model using this cue to help you say the dialogue correctly. Ask the children to read some dialogue to their partner.

◢ Review

- Give children time to rehearse their reading-aloud skills. Let them become very familiar with a story so they can put emotion, intonation and expression into their reading. Explain that if they find clues that tell us a character is shy, bossy, old or young, for example, then they could create a voice that shows these attributes. Practice making up voices with the children to really bring dialogue to life.

◢ Watch and listen

- Listen for children swiftly using their comprehension of a text to inform the way that they read it aloud.

- Watch out for children who can read dialogue with appropriate expression as this shows inference beyond basic understanding. Children who can read at this level are fluent enough readers to take notice of the characters' feelings. They can comprehend as they read and can make judgements about the tone and expression they are using to show their understanding.

9

Objectives

- To answer and ask questions.
- To discuss their understanding of books, poems and other material.

What the children need to know

- The key aspects of a story: plot, character and setting.
- How to identify the basic facts of a story.
- How to find key ideas in a section of the story.

TEST LINKS:

Test 1: Q3, 5, 9, 10, 11, 12, 13, 14, 15, 16
Test 3: Q1, 2, 3, 4, 5, 6, 7, 8, 9, 10, 11, 12, 13, 15, 16, 17
Test 4: Q1, 2, 3, 4, 5, 6, 7, 8, 9, 10, 11, 12, 13
Test 6: Q 2, 3, 4, 5, 6, 7, 8, 9, 10, 11, 12, 13, 14
Test 8: Q3, 5, 6, 7

WORKBOOK LINKS:

Pages 33–35

The features of fiction

✈ Challenge and mastery ideas

- Ensure children have a solid understanding of the events of each story they read before going deeper into the text. (Use the sequencing and retelling activities ideas on pages 36–44 of the *Workbook* for further support.)
- Remember together a handful of favourite stories, for example, 'Cinderella' or 'Little Red Riding Hood' or well-known picture books such as *The Gruffalo*, by Julia Donaldson or *We're Going on a Bear Hunt*, by Michael Rosen. Encourage the children to help you write the key aspects of each story. Ask them to find the main characters and the different settings. Make links between the plot and the settings, and then add in the characters.
- Provide the children with individual copies of photocopiable page 45 'Plot, character, setting'. Ask them to choose three favourite stories and fill in the main characters (for example, Fox, Mouse, Owl, Gruffalo, Snake), the setting (the wood) and key events from the story (for example: a mouse lives in a wood; the mouse tells a fox, a snake and an owl that he is going to have dinner with a gruffalo; the Gruffalo follows the mouse through the woods; all the animals become scared of the mouse).
- If you have a picture book you can display on a whiteboard, choose one paragraph of the story and discuss how to underline or highlight the main ideas in that section. Ask the children to discuss what new information they gained about the story by reading that paragraph.

✈ Review

- Some questions will ask children to find multiple pieces of information in a text. Ensure the children read the question carefully so they know exactly what they need to find.

✈ Watch and listen

- Watch out for children who can understand that each aspect of the story impacts on other parts of the story. Ask the children to think about how each paragraph in the story builds on information from previous parts of the story. Ask them to consider what would happen if one part of the story changed – how would it impact on the later parts of the story?
- Children who can hold character, plot and settings in their heads as they read will be able to read longer books and retain vital information from earlier parts of the story, which enables them to enjoy more complicated characterisation and plots.

10 Retelling stories

Objectives

- To retell a wider range of stories, fairy stories and traditional tales.
- To understand the books they read by drawing on what they already know or on background vocabulary.

What the children need to know

- A wide range of fairy tales and traditional tales.
- A wide range of classic children's picture books.
- Adverbial and prepositional language to create order when retelling a story.

WORKBOOK LINKS:
Pages 36–39

✈ Challenge and mastery ideas

- Ensure that the children have a wide range of stories to draw on by reading traditional tales, fairy tales and classic children's literature. The wider their knowledge of stories the more they will be able to connect to the stories they are retelling.
- Help the children understand story structure by using story maps or by 'boxing up' the events in a story, as in the example below. (You might like to direct the children to their completed versions of photocopiable page 45.)

> 1 The billy goats want to cross the bridge.

> 2 The troll wants to eat the smallest billy goat. But the smallest billy goat persuades him to eat his brother.

> 3 The middle billy goat does the same as his little brother.

> 4 The biggest billy goat butts the troll off the bridge and so all the billy goats cross the bridge.

- Encourage the children to plan for their retelling by drawing a story map and then rehearsing and retelling their story a few times before sharing it.
- Model using prepositional phrases and adverbial clauses to move the retelling of stories on, for example: *later on, after that, once she had found the, all at once, soon* and so on. Encourage the children to decide where they could use one of these phrases and to add it to their story map.
- Show the children how to add additional detail to describe characters and settings and, when they are more confident, how to add characters' feelings to add depth to their story retelling.

✈ Review

- Ask children to retell their stories. As they do, listen out for accurate and full descriptions of key characters, a clear understanding of the sequence of events and a succinct description of the main setting.

✈ Watch and listen

- Look out for children who can retain all the basic information about a story and integrate prepositional and adverbial language as they retell the story.
- Watch out for children with the ability to orchestrate their knowledge of a story with pertinent details: they are working at a sophisticated level.
- Watch out for reuse of appropriate stock descriptions of characters that are used in fairy and traditional tales such as *the bad-tempered giant, the daring prince, the resourceful girl*.
- Look out for children who can use contrast to describe characters: *she was poor but still she was generous*.

11 Sequencing stories

Objectives

- To discuss the sequence of events in books and how items of information are related.
- To explain and discuss their understanding of books.
- To predict what might happen on the basis of what has been read so far.

What the children need to know

- That a series of events make up a story.
- That these events are interconnected.
- That a character's behaviour can be predicted by looking at how they behaved in similar circumstances.

TEST LINKS:

Test 1: Q10, 16
Test 4: Q13
Test 6: Q13
Test 8: Q5

WORKBOOK LINKS:
Pages 40–44

Challenge and mastery ideas

- The ability to sequence events in stories is a key reading skill. Being able to recall the order of events in longer stories and make links to characters' previous actions enables children to enjoy books where events are interlinked over many chapters.
- Share the story on photocopiable pages 46–47 'The Golden Goose'. Encourage the children to summarise each event in turn.
- Ask the children to use their understanding of what happens in stories to people who generously share what they have to predict whether the old man will help Jack in some way.
- Talk about other stories involving Jack (for example, 'Jack in the Beanstalk'). Agree that good things often happen to Jack.
- Ask the children to consider how each event in the story helps them to get to know the characters, plot and likely outcomes better. Pause to ask: *What do you think is going to happen to the lady who sells ribbons?*
- Help the children remember the sequence of chapter books that they read by modelling how to recap what has happened in a book so far before they read a new chapter.
- As children move on to read longer books, they may at first find the leap into stories broken up into extended sequential episodes tricky. Help them to keep a track of characters by making quick verbal summaries about them and what they have done in the story so far.
- Teach the children about patterns that emerge in stories: how one character who makes a sacrifice might get their reward or a character who behaves selfishly might get their comeuppance later on in the story.

Review

- Ask the children to retell a version of 'The Golden Goose'. Can they remember the sequence of events?

Watch and listen

- Watch for children who are now confidently reading chapter books.
- Look out for children who begin to make predictions about stories linked to this deeper understanding of story structure.

12

Making links to other books

Objectives

- To make links between the book they are reading and other books they have read.
- To understand the books they read by drawing on what they already know or on background information.

What the children need to know

- That stories have common themes.
- That stories can be broadly categorised, for example: fairy tales, science fiction, funny stories, fantasy stories, and so on.
- That books can reflect their own experiences.

WORKBOOK LINKS:

Pages 45–47

✈ Challenge and mastery ideas

- As you read aloud to your class, make links to other stories the children will know. After reading, ask questions such as: *X was brave, wasn't she? Which other character does she remind you of? Although this story was set on the moon, it really reminded me of another story. Which story did it remind you of? How do you think the story would change if X behaved more like Little Red Riding Hood?*
- Gather a bundle of picture books together and ask the children to sort the books into categories – these can be totally fluid and decided by the children. When they have sorted their bundle of books, ask the children to explain to the rest of the class how they have sorted the books.
- Make links between longer chapter books and the picture books, fairy tales and traditional tales that the children are familiar with.
- Help children make recommendations of books to younger children based on the books that the younger children enjoy.
- Provide the children with photocopiable page 48 'That reminds me'. Ask the children to work in small groups. Ask each group to choose a story and write the title in the central bubble and the plot, character and setting information in the circles. Ask them to work together to think of other stories (including stories and characters they know from films) that have similar characters, plots or settings as the story in the centre.

✈ Review

- Making links to other books is not an expectation of the Reading Test, however it is one way that children can demonstrate they are working at greater depth. Ask the children to talk to you about the books they are reading and encourage them to reflect on how they are similar to other books they have read.
- Ask the children to write a book report on a story and include who would enjoy the story, for example, 'fans of Harry Potter' or 'readers who like funny stories'.

✈ Watch and listen

- Gather evidence of children's wider reading by asking them to consider what one character might do in another's position. Watch for children who can think flexibly and make sensible predictions about the character as this shows a deep connection to both stories.
- Listen for children who can discuss ideas and themes that run across books. Have book-club-style discussions with open questions for these children, such as: *I really like the princess in this book – she didn't wait to be rescued; have you read any books with girl characters that are strong like this one is?*

13

Making predictions

Objectives

- To predict what might happen on the basis of what they have read so far.
- To become familiar with fairy stories and traditional tales.
- To make inferences on the basis of what is being said and done.

What the children need to know

- How to make predictions about how a character might behave from clues in the text.
- How to make connections between a story they know and other stories.
- How to link their knowledge of stories and stock characters to help make likely predictions.
- Use inferences to predict what is likely to happen next.

TEST LINKS:

Test 4: Q12
Test 8: Q9

WORKBOOK LINKS:
Pages 48–50

✐ Challenge and mastery ideas

- Predictions are a form of inference. They rely on the reader making connections between the story they are reading and other stories they have encountered. Children need a wide story store so they can make accurate predictions.
- Accurate predictions are based on children understanding how stories are typically structured and how characters typically behave. Reinforce the children's knowledge of the main structures of stories by making story maps that show:
  - a circular story, for example, *Oi! Get off our Train* by John Burningham
  - a dilemma story, for example, 'Beauty and the Beast'
  - a quest story, for example, *Beegu* by Alexis Deacon
  - a rags-to-riches story, for example, 'Cinderella'.
- Help children to predict how characters might behave or how the story may unfold through modelling how to find clues about the genre of story that they are reading. Make sure that you identify key features of stories (such as the rule of three in fairy tales – things happen in threes.) so that the children are alert to these features and can use them when they read.
- Prediction relies on a strong understanding of character and story arcs. Ensure the children can talk about these aspects of story. Model talking about characters and their actions. Explain when you are surprised by a character's behaviour or plot twist. Teach the children how to actively read by questioning characters' motives and actions.
- Read stories with cliffhangers to the children. Ask them to predict how the character will get out of the trouble they are in!

✐ Review

- Provide the children with copies of photocopiable page 49 'What happened next?'. Ask the children to write their prediction for what would happen next. Look for the children's understanding of the stock fairy-tale character and modern-day story themes to make their choice. Challenge some children to explain why they made their choice.

✐ Watch and listen

- Watch out for children who can predict how a story would change if it were told from another character's point of view.
- Use humorous retellings of well-known stories and fairy tales. Look out for children who can predict how the character will alter the story, or describe other characters so they look good.

14

Understanding description

Objectives

- To recognise simple, recurring literary language in stories and poetry.

What the children need to know

- Writers use special techniques to help readers imagine characters and setting more clearly.
- Techniques can be used to create different effects.

TEST LINKS:

Test 3: Q1, 4, 7, 9, 11, 13, 15, 16, 17
Test 4: Q2

WORKBOOK LINKS:

Pages 51–54

✈ Challenge and mastery ideas

- Use poems that have similes and onomatopoeia to help children see how these devices create vivid images. (Note, children do not need to know these terms but you can choose to introduce them if appropriate.)
- Use the poem 'Owls' on photocopiable page 50 to identify similes and onomatopoeia.
- Show children how to identify a simile by looking out for the words 'like' and 'as' being used to compare two things. (You can choose to use the term 'simile' or not, depending on the needs of your group.)
- Discuss how the similes in the poem 'Owls' help the children to see owls in a new way. Ask the children to discuss what they see when they read the similes.
- Ask the children to use the poem to draw how they see the owls in their mind's eye. Encourage them to choose a part that they have really connected with.
- Explain that some words make sounds: the word *sizzle* sounds a lot like something sizzling. In this poem, there are lots of words that make sounds, for example *hoots*. Ask the children to underline any examples of onomatopoeia.
- Play with other onomatopoeic words – create a wall of sound words. Watch out for other onomatopoeic words in the books you read.
- Model how to use these words to help enliven children's reading aloud.

✈ Review

- Ensure that the children are picking up on literary devices in any word-based questions.

✈ Watch and listen

- Look out for children who can understand how the writer creates images by combining ideas. Similes and metaphors require children to deeply engage in what they are reading, and children need robust vocabularies to fully enjoy them.
- Watch for children who are able to talk about these devices. Challenge children by teasing out the images and ideas created by similes and metaphors they have met in their reading. Help children think out loud about the ideas these devices bring up for them. Develop their thinking by asking them if the simile or metaphor works for them. What new idea or image has it given them?

15

Inference: what characters say, do and think

Objectives
- To make inferences on the basis of what is said and done.

What the children need to know
- That characters don't always do what they say they will.
- How to make predictions about a character's behaviour based on their previous actions.
- To locate clues about characters and plot 'hidden' in stories.
- How to empathise with characters.
- That characters might behave differently in different situations.

TEST LINKS:

Test 1: Q2, 5, 11, 12, 13, 14, 15
Test 3: Q2, 7, 9, 11, 13,15, 16, 17
Test 4: Q3, 5, 10, 11, 12
Test 5: Q10, 12, 15
Test 6: Q4, 5, 7, 8, 11, 12
Test 7: Q6, 7, 9, 10, 11
Test 8: Q3, 7, 9, 10, 11, 12, 13, 14

WORKBOOK LINKS:
Pages 55–57

◄ Challenge and mastery ideas

- Ask the children to tell you everything they know about the Big Bad Wolf in 'Little Red Riding Hood' and the 'Three Little Pigs'. Note down the children's ideas.

- Ask the children to tell you how they know these things about the Big Bad Wolf – what is their evidence from the story? Encourage them to consider what the Wolf says and what the Wolf does. Divide their feedback into actions and dialogue; for example, *I know he is cunning because he has a plan to distract Little Red Riding Hood so he can get to Grandmother's house first.*

- Repeat this process with other characters from the stories. Remind the children that in some versions of the stories, the Big Bad Wolf – although he is still a 'baddie' – is outwitted by the Little Pigs and Little Red Riding Hood.

- Ask the children to consider how the Big Bad Wolf sees himself. Do they think that other characters see the Wolf in the same way? Challenge the children to think of how Little Red Riding Hood might see the Wolf as dangerous rather than cunning, and why this might be. Provide the children with photocopiable page 51 'Good wolf, bad wolf' on which to record their thoughts.

- Challenge the children to use the photocopiable page for another character that they know well.

- Explain that characters are not always honest – they might say one thing and think something entirely different – for example, what do they think the Wolf is thinking when he says: *'Little Pig, Little Pig, let me come in.'*

- Ask the children to consider what would happen if a character behaved differently in a story they know well. Ask: *How would the story change if Little Red Riding Hood stayed on the path or if the Wolf was really trying to be friends with the Three Little Pigs? Which aspects of the story would change?*

- Ask questions such as: *What if the Wolf were scared – how would be behave? What if the ugly stepsisters were kind – how would Cinderella's life be different?*

- Ask the children to consider how the setting affects the story. Ask: *How would the story of 'Cinderella' change if it were to happen in the future or now?*

- Read passages of story where characters' emotions are signalled by how they speak or behave. Direct children to the words that *show* but don't *tell* how a character is feeling, for example: *When it says 'the stepmother sneered when she said Cinderella couldn't go to the ball' I know she is feeling delight at Cinderella's misfortune.*

- Model reading the dialogue out loud to show a character's emotion. Can the children work out how the character is feeling? Write a list of words that can be used to describe speech that shows emotions, for example: *snivelled*, *muttered*, *grumbled*, *soothed*, and so on.
- Explain to the children how the verbs used by the writer can show how a character is feeling. Model slumping, dragging your feet, dawdling and so on, and ask the children to think how these movements show emotions too. Write a list of verbs that can be used to show how a character is feeling.

◤ Review

- Provide the children with copies of photocopiable pages 46–47 'The Golden Goose'. Ask: 1. *How do Jack, the ribbon seller and the princess feel? How do you know? 2. What sort of character is Jack? What sort of character is the milkmaid? How do you know?*

◤ Watch and listen

- Look out for children who understand that characters need to present a less-than-truthful version of themselves at times. Children who can recognise character types will be able to predict their behaviour and uncover the motivations of their actions more easily. Develop this by encouraging children to make links between characters in different books.
- Watch out for children who can empathise with characters; these children will not only enjoy the story more – because they are making a deeper connection – but will also be able to make more accurate inferences as they read. Ask questions to develop empathy, such as: *What would you do in that character's place? How would you solve that problem if you were that character? Do you think that character made the right decision? How do you think the character feels now?*

16

Fiction: your opinion

Objectives

- To express views about a wide range of contemporary and classic poetry, stories and non-fiction.

What the children need to know

- How they feel about a character based on what they have read.
- How to find evidence about whether a character behaved fairly or not.
- To be able to imagine what it would be like to make the same decisions as a character.

✈ Challenge and mastery ideas

- Explain to the children that we might not like all the characters that we meet in books. Some characters are written in such a way that they are hard to like. Some characters are baddies and it is fun to dislike them. Can they think of characters that they have really liked and give their reasons why? Ask the children to think of characters they didn't like and give their reasons why.

- Tell the children that an opinion is a judgement that someone has made about something. People use the evidence that they have to help them come to a decision. For example, some people might think that the Wolf in 'The Three Little Pigs' is just doing what wolves do – chasing and eating prey; some other people might think that the Wolf is bad for doing this. These are opinions: neither person is wrong. They both have their reasons for what they think and can explain them. Challenge the children to think of some good reasons why baddies in the books they have read behaved the way they did.

- Ask the children to think about some of the characters in the books that they have read who behaved badly. *Was Max in* Where the Wild Things Are (by Maurice Sendak) *a good king? Why? Was the bear in* We're Going on a Bear Hunt (by Michael Rosen) *dangerous? Why or why not?*

✈ Review

- Support children in forming appropriate opinions that are backed up with evidence from the text when they are asked *What do you think...?*

✈ Watch and listen

- Look out for children who can empathise with characters and see that sometimes it is hard to make the right choice in a story.

- Watch out for children who can articulate why they do or don't like a character and refer to the story as evidence. Support children by modelling how to use the text to back up their opinion, for example: *I feel that Max in* Where the Wild Things Are *is mean and selfish when he tells the Wild Things that he won't be their king anymore.*

TEST LINKS:

Test 1: Q12, 13, 15
Test 6: Q14

WORKBOOK LINKS:
Pages 58–60

17 Reading non-fiction

Objectives

- To be introduced to non-fiction books that are structured in different ways.
- To answer and ask questions.
- To discuss their understanding of books, poems and other material.

What the children need to know

- How to quickly work out what a text is about.
- How to find key words and ideas.
- How to sum up the information they have found.

◢ Challenge and mastery ideas

- Ensure children have a solid understanding of the key ideas or concepts in the text before going deeper.
- Ensure they understand the technical language and the way that common words might be used differently in the non-fiction context.
- Encourage the children to help you identify the main ideas in the texts you read. Ask them to find the titles, headings and captions, and discuss how these give the reader useful pointers about the information that is coming next.
- Choose one paragraph of the story and discuss how to underline or highlight the main ideas and key words in that section. Ask the children to discuss what new information they have gained by reading that paragraph.

◢ Review

- Provide the children with photocopiable page 52 'The hippopotamus'. Ask them to locate the main title, the photograph, the subheading, two key words and to say in one sentence what the text is about.

◢ Watch and listen

- Watch for children who can summarise the main ideas from a sentence or paragraph. Encourage children to use their own words, where possible, so you can be sure that they fully comprehend the text.
- Look out for children who independently realise that some words have different meanings in the non-fiction context. Encourage children to underline words they are unsure of and help them understand how to use a dictionary to find the appropriate definition.

TEST LINKS:

Test 2: Q2, 3, 4, 5, 6, 7, 8, 9, 10, 11, 12, 13
Test 5: Q1, 3, 4, 5, 6, 7, 8, 9, 10, 11, 12, 13, 14, 15
Test 7: Q2, 3, 4, 5, 6, 7, 8, 9, 10, 11

WORKBOOK LINKS:
Pages 61–64

18

Links in non-fiction

Objectives

- To understand how items of information are related.

What the children need to know

- To understand how ideas build upon each other.
- To recognise a topic sentence that introduces an idea.
- To find key words that are linked to each other.

Challenge and mastery ideas

- Explain to the children that information texts are organised in such a way that ideas are linked and built upon in each paragraph. Provide the children with copies of photocopiable page 52 'The hippopotamus'. Ask them to identify the topic sentence that introduces the main idea for the text. Show children how to find and underline the key words and summarise the main idea into one sentence. (Carried out on page 35 in the 'Review' section). Now provide them with photocopiable page 53 'Key words and ideas' and ask the children to fill in the boxes.

- Look at other non-fiction texts and discuss how explanations break down an idea or process into steps so the reader can understand how something works. Ask the children to think about the order of the information. Ask: *Does the order make a difference to understanding how something works?*

- Cut up the paragraphs from a new non-fiction text. Ask the children to try to put them in order. Give them the original text to compare with their answers. Ask: *Does the order matter?* Discuss the types of words and phrases that help link ideas and the words that create cohesion.

Review

- Provide the children with a new non-fiction text at their reading age and a fresh copy of photocopiable page 53. Ask the children to complete the photocopiable page for the new text.

Watch and listen

- Watch out for children who can make links between pieces of information over a series of paragraphs. Encourage children to look back when they are reading non-fiction texts to think about how one paragraph is linked to another. Can any of the children sum up the main idea of a paragraph? Being able to quickly sum up ideas and see how they build through a text is a sign of a confident reader who is fully engaged with the subject they are reading.

TEST LINKS:

Test 2: Q7, 8
Test 5: Q8, 10, 13, 14
Test 7: Q9, 10, 11

WORKBOOK LINKS:
Pages 65–67

19

Making an explanation: fiction and non-fiction

Objectives
- To explain and discuss their understanding of books, poems and other material.

What the children need to know
- How to put a sequence of events in order.
- To be able to say how or why something happens.
- To make connections between actions and consequences.

TEST LINKS:

Test 1: Q12, 13
Test 2: Q13
Test 4: Q10, 11, 12
Test 5: Q12, 15
Test 6: Q5, 7, 14
Test 8: Q14

WORKBOOK LINKS:
Pages 68–73

✈ Challenge and mastery ideas

- Explaining ideas requires children to bring many ideas together and then put them into a logical order. Give the children something that they are very familiar with as a starting point. For example, ask them to explain to a partner why they have break times at school.

- Give children scenarios from stories they know well. For example, ask the children to explain how 'Traction Man' feels when he gets a knitted green suit from granny for Christmas. Can they explain the reasons for the character feeling the way they do? Make sure they refer to the text – this will help them improve their inference skills too.

- Give the children a variety of information texts with explanations as well as information. Ask the children to circle the explanations. Ask: *How are they structured differently to information or instructions?*

- Show children how to use the word 'because' to create explanations. For example: *We see the stars at night because it is dark. The stars are always in the sky but we can't see them in the daylight because of the glare of the sunlight.*

✈ Review

- Provide the children with a simple explanation text at their reading age. Ask them to summarise the text into three circles. The first circle should contain the fact that is being explained, the second should be the word 'because' and the third circle should include a simple version of the explanation.

✈ Watch and listen

- Watch out for children who can make connections between the information they read and the bigger ideas. Can they refer to evidence in the text when they make their explanation?

- Look out for children who can make logical links between information that may be given in separate paragraphs.

Root word challenge

Cut up these words into root word and prefix (**un**, **in**, **dis**, **im**, **non**).

Look at each word in turn.

Muddle up the root words and prefixes. Try adding the prefixes to different root words. Can you make any new words?

imbalance	incredible
unleash	undrunk
unpopular	dissimilar
intolerant	disbelief
independent	discontinue
disregard	disgrace
disarm	insane
unfair	unkind
dislike	immature
nonsense	inefficient

Compound words

Can you work out the meaning of these compound words?

First, draw a line to split the compound word into the two words that have been used to create it.

Then, using the meaning of the words you know to work out the meaning of the compound word and explain it to your partner.

whiteboard	cheesecake
horsefly	wheelchair
soundproof	backbone
mouthpiece	doorstop
battleship	motorbike
honeypot	downpour
drainpipe	blackbird
skyscraper	candlestick
cheesecloth	spaceship
timetable	skateboard

Homophones

Cut out these words to create word cards. Place the cards in a hat.
Take turns to pick out a card and explain its meaning.

piece	eight	too
peace	blew	two
they're	blue	hole
their	flour	whole
there	flower	one
here	wear	won
hear	where	plain
it's	sale	plane
its	sail	tale
chews	allowed	tail
choose	aloud	read
ate	to	red

Synonym snap

Cut out the word cards and shuffle them.

Use the cards to play a game of 'Snap' with your partner. A snap is when one player puts down a card with a similar meaning to the card the previous player has just put down.

sprint	hot	fierce	funny
dash	roasting	ferocious	comic
speed	boiling	savage	hilarious
rocket	stuffy	beastly	amusing
cold	old	gentle	amazing
chilly	ancient	kind	fantastic
freezing	historic	tender	wonderful
bitter	elderly	loving	superb

The right word

Write the words into the correct box.
Note: Some words might go in both boxes!

splendid   meek

lonely   determined

miserable   rushing

clever   scary

flexible   isolated

excited   difficult

ridiculous   troublesome

industrious   thoughtful

exotic   spectacular

Words to describe things

Words to describe people

Syllable snips

Read these words.

Use a line to mark the syllables.

Circle any parts of the words you are not sure about.

garden	circle	pleasure
thunder	invention	mission
follow	invitation	complete
sudden	magician	rescue
difficult	question	suddenly
different	special	escape
disappear	explosion	computer
marvellous	treasure	adventure
mysterious	creature	mixture
naughty	somewhere	everywhere
afternoon	mystery	

With feeling

Read the sentences and think about the emotions.
What feeling does the exclamation mark stand for?
Write your answer on the line.

1. Chocolate cake is the best dessert!

_____

2. I hate it when it rains and I am stuck inside!

_____

3. I wish I could draw as well as Rani!

_____

4. The Three Little Pigs could hardly believe their eyes when the wolf ran run away!

_____

5. Watch out if adding vinegar to baking powder as it can explode!

_____

6. Be quiet!

_____

7. Help, I'm stuck!

_____

8. The present was a big disappointment!

_____

Plot, character, setting

Think of three of your favourite stories.
Fill in the chart.

	1.	2.	3.
Name of story			
Main characters			
Setting			
Four things that happen — 1.			
2.			
3.			
4.			

The Golden Goose (1)

Once upon a time, there was a young man called Jack. Jack was very silly but kind-hearted. One day, Jack's mother sent him into the woods to chop wood.

In the woods, he met a little old man.

"Hello," said Jack. "Would you like to share my bread with me?" "Yes," said the man. "Thank you. And then I will help you cut down that tree over there."

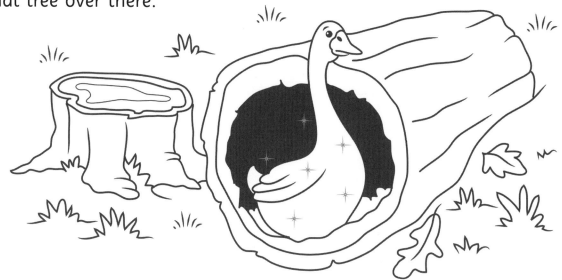

When the little old man and Jack cut down the tree – my, oh, my – inside the tree stump was a goose with feathers made of pure gold. Jack turned to the little old man but he was gone. Jack picked up the goose and started to walk home.

As Jack passed a field of cows, a milkmaid saw the goose and secretly tried to steal a feather. But as soon as she touched it – BAM – she was stuck solid. Jack looked at the girl in horror. The milkmaid's two sisters tried to pull the girl off the goose and – BAM – they were stuck too. Jack kept on walking home, and the girls had to run to keep up.

Jack, the goose and the girls went through the market. A lady selling ribbons saw the goose and went to stroke it – BAM – she became stuck too! She screamed with shock and her husband came to help. BAM! He became stuck to his wife. The street-cleaner and the baker came to help and soon they were stuck with their arms around the ribbon-seller's husband.

Jack ran into the countryside and past the castle. The princess was looking out of the window and saw Jack, the goose, the milkmaid and her sisters, the ribbon seller and her husband, the street cleaner and the baker, and she laughed. She laughed and laughed until there were tears rolling down her face. "I will marry that fool!" she said. And she did.

That reminds me

Write the name of your favourite story in the middle box.

Fill in the other bubbles with other stories, characters and settings that are like your first story.

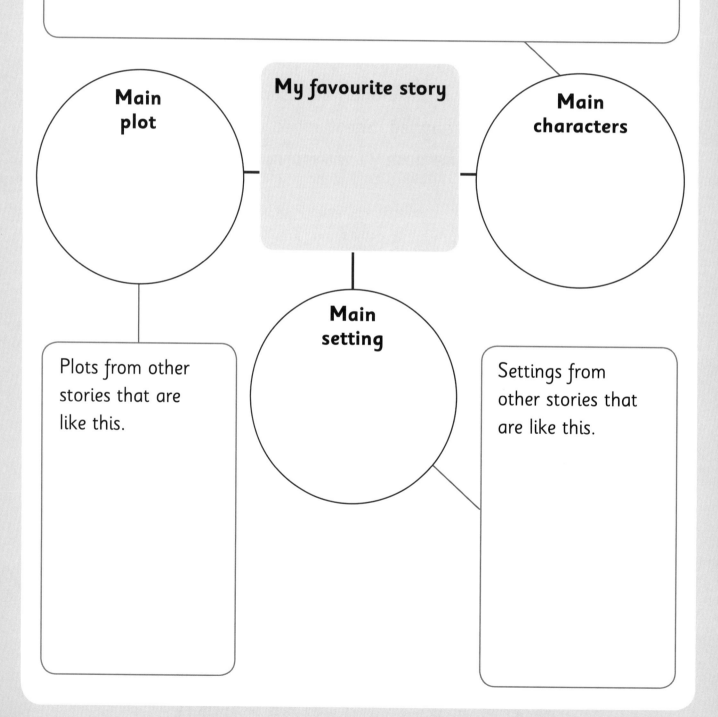

Characters from other stories that are like these.

Main plot

My favourite story

Main characters

Main setting

Plots from other stories that are like this.

Settings from other stories that are like this.

What happened next?

Look at each scene. Choose what happened next.
You can choose one of the ideas or write your own.

What happened next?
The old lady refused the food.
The old lady gave her three wishes.

My idea _____

_____

_____

_____

What happened next?
The boy fell into the water.
The boy pulls himself up the rope.

My idea _____

_____

_____

_____

_____

What happened next?
He is told to put the puppy back.
He hides the puppy under his bed.

My idea _____

_____

_____

_____

Read the poem.

Draw a picture next to a part of the poem that you really liked.

Owls

Swift and silent as night falling

The owl glides over the fields

Its face as white as any ghost

As it calls and hoots and shrieks.

This owl that perches high above us,

Like a statue made of soft terror

Waits...

For it, time does not matter.

That owl, who nesting, calls another

To swoop, and dip, and hunt, and kill

To feed their babies, that, like balls of hunger,

Cry and wail and squeak and shrill.

But the owls – they do not care for us,

They are hunters in the night,

We are merely watchers,

Witnessing their delight!

By Charlotte Raby

Good wolf, bad wolf

What do you think of the Big Bad Wolf and Cinderella? Fill in the chart with your thoughts.

Then think of another fairy-tale character and fill in the chart for them.

Character 1: Big Bad Wolf	Character 2: Cinderella	Your character:
Rival: Little Red Riding Hood	Rival: The Stepmother	Your character's rival:
What does the Big Bad Wolf think about himself?	What does Cinderella think about herself?	What does your character think about himself or herself?
What does Little Red Riding Hood think of the Big Bad Wolf?	What does the Stepmother think of Cinderella?	What does the rival think about your character?

The hippopotamus

The hippopotamus is a large herbivore that lives in Africa. Its name means 'river horse'. Hippos have some similar features to pigs, but in fact they are more closely related to whales and dolphins!

Living together

Hippos live in pods with one bull male in charge of many female and young hippos. They need to be near water all the time: they spend most of the day keeping cool in the water and mud. They can stay underwater for up to 5 minutes. They leave the water each night to graze on grasses.

Fast runners

Despite their short legs and large barrel-like bodies, hippos are fast runners and can charge at an amazing 30 kilometres per hour.

Key words and ideas

Write down the main ideas in a piece of non-fiction text.

1. Circle the topic sentence that introduces the non-fiction text.
2. Underline the key words in the text.
3. Fill in the boxes below to show the five main points in the text. Put a key word and short main idea in each one.

Key word: _____

Idea: _____

_____

_____

Key word: _____

Idea: _____

_____

_____

Key word: _____

Idea: _____

_____

_____

Key word: _____

Idea: _____

_____

_____

Key word: _____

Idea: _____

_____

_____

Notes

Notes

Send your skills into orbit

ADDITIONAL SUPPORT FOR THE NATIONAL TESTS

TARGETED PREPARATION TO BUILD CONFIDENCE

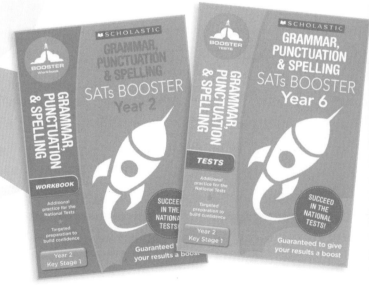

Guaranteed to give **your** results a boost!